JUSTIN BIEBER

Liz Gogerly

SEA-TO-SEA
Mankato   Collingwood   London

This edition first published in 2013 by
Sea-to-Sea Publications
Distributed by Black Rabbit Books
P.O. Box 3263, Mankato, Minnesota 56002

Copyright © Sea-to-Sea Publications 2013

Printed in the United States of America, North Mankato, MN

9 8 7 6 5 4 3 2

Published by arrangement with the Watts Publishing Group Ltd, London.

Library of Congress Cataloging-in-Publication Data

Gogerly, Liz.
  Justin Bieber / written by Liz Gogerly.
      pages cm – (Teen stars)
  Includes index.
  ISBN 978-1-59771-415-0 (hardcover, library bound)
  1. Bieber, Justin, 1994–Juvenile literature. 2. Singers–Canada–Biography–Juvenile literature.
  I. Title.
  ML3930.B54G64 2013
  782.42164092–dc23
  [B]
                              2012002537

Series Editor: Adrian Cole
Art Direction: Peter Scoulding
Design: Simon Borrough
Picture Research: Diana Morris

Acknowledgements:
Aeg Live/Insurge Pictures/Island Def Jam/Mtv Film/Kobal Collection: 27.
AFP/Miguel Ruiz/Getty Images: 20. Agencia EFE/Rex Features: front cover, 17.
BDG/Rex Features: 18. Larry Busacca/Getty Images: 23.
Rick Diamond/Getty Images: 6. Helga Esteb/Shutterstock: 4.
David Fisher/Rex Features: 29. Charles Gallay/WireImages/Getty Images: 12.
Dave Hogan/Getty Images: 16. KeystoneUSA-ZUMA/Rex Features: 25.
Kevin Mazur/WireImages /Getty Images: 5, 24.
Heathcliff O'Malley/Rex Features: 7. Cindy Ord/Getty Images: 10.
George Pimentel/Getty Images: 8. Jo Seer/Shutterstock: 19.
Irving Shuter/Getty Images: 11. Jim Smeal/BEI/Rex Features: 15.
Startraks/Rex Features: 14. Adam Taylor/© ABC/Getty Images: 28.
Noel Vasquez/Getty Images: 21. Kevin Winter/Getty Images: 13, 22.

Every attempt has been made to clear copyright. Should there be any
inadvertent omission please apply to the publisher for rectification.

RD/6000006415/001
May 2012

Contents

Words highlighted in the text can be found in the glossary.

You Better Bebieber It!

Justin Bieber is the number-one pop heartthrob. The young Canadian singer-songwriter, musician, and budding actor is probably the most talked about teen on the planet.

Justin is often dubbed "the first Internet pop sensation." Millions of Justin's fans first clapped eyes on him on YouTube in 2007. By 2008, Justin was signed up by singer-songwriter Usher's record label. The reigning King of **R&B** supports Justin and has been there to help him during his incredible rise to fame.

Justin's first single—"One Time"—was released in 2009. It was an international hit. In 2010, Justin won Artist of the Year at the American Music Awards. To top it all off, he became the most Googled name on the Internet, a position previously held by Lady Gaga!

Justin with his shorter hairstyle first seen in 2011.

4

Usher said, "He's a young man who I think represents all of what's needed in this time to be an artist and be successful ..."

Born to Be Somebody

Justin was born on March 1, 1994, in London, Ontario, Canada. His mom, Pattie Mallette, was just 18 at the time. Justin's dad, Jeremy Jack Bieber, walked out on the family when Justin was a baby.

Justin and his mom at the CMT Music Awards in 2011.

Justin was raised in the town of Stratford, Ontario. After the divorce, Pattie worked hard doing low-paid office jobs. Pattie's strong Christian faith helped her through the difficult times.

Pattie, Justin, and Justin the waxwork look-alike figure.

He may be an only child, but Justin grew up surrounded by love. He was close to his grandparents. His father Jeremy moved to Winnipeg in Manitoba, Canada, but kept in regular contact. Justin credits his dad with teaching him how to drive.

"The day I was born, March 1, 1994, Celine Dion was solid at number 1 with 'The Power of Love.' Not a bad start to your life."

Justin's dad Jeremy married again and now has a young family. Justin has a stepsister, Jazmyn (born in 2008), and stepbrother, Jaxon (born in 2009). Justin is close to his cute little siblings.

Groovy Guitar Boy

Music has always been a part of Justin's life. When most kids are learning to walk and talk, Justin was playing drums and picking up a guitar.

Justin plays guitar live on stage at a concert in 2009.

Justin's mother, Pattie Mallette, said, "I always knew Justin was gifted. Even as a one-year-old who was barely standing, I remember him banging on tables, banging in rhythm."

Justin's mother loves music, too. At home, she played her favorite R&B tracks and sang along to bands like Boyz II Men. By the age of eight, Justin was teaching himself to play the guitar.

Justin is left-handed but he first learned to play on a right-handed guitar. He had to keep switching it around to play.

Justin remembers his dad teaching him some songs. One of his favorites was "Knocking on Heaven's Door" by Bob Dylan. As well as the guitar, Justin taught himself to play the piano, the drums, and the trumpet. Before long he could play along to the music of **soul** superstars such as Michael Jackson and Aretha Franklin.

The Kid  Has It!

Justin was 12 years old when he got up and sang Aretha Franklin's "Respect" at a local singing contest. He came second place in the competition, but it was a turning point in his life ...

Justin's mom filmed her son's performance on a video camera. The quality of the film was terrible, but she uploaded it onto YouTube. Pattie wanted the family to see her boy in action.

Justin on top of the Empire State Building in New York.

Justin **busked** on the streets of his hometown Stratford (below). A passerby filmed him singing there when he was 12. The video has been watched over 3.2 million times on YouTube.

66 **Music is music, and I'm definitely influenced by Michael Jackson and Boyz II Men and [other] black artists. But I like their voices and I like how they entertain—it's not about what color they are.** 99

Before long, thousands of people were watching Justin on YouTube. Pattie encouraged Justin to get in front of the camera again and again. At the time, Justin did cover songs of stars such as Alicia Keys and Ne-Yo. As each new song was uploaded to YouTube, loads more people began to follow him.

11

Mega
Record Deal

It wasn't long before music managers were on Justin's trail. Some of the top names in the business called his mother. But Pattie was no pushover. She didn't trust people in the music industry.

It took talent manager "Scooter" Braun to change Pattie's mind. In 2008, Scooter watched footage of Justin on YouTube by accident. He recognized major talent when he saw it. When he finally got through to Pattie on the telephone, they talked for hours. Scooter convinced her to fly out with Justin to Atlanta to record some **demos**—Justin was 13 years old.

Justin and Scooter at Scooter's 30th birthday party in June 2011.

Usher said, "The day I met Justin was special. I saw that he had a raw talent—and he was cute, girls would like him. I thought OK, if this is properly nourished it could become huge."

Justin performs with Usher at the GRAMMY Awards in 2011.

In Atlanta, Scooter introduced Justin to Usher. Usher had been signed to a record label at 14 years old. Scooter thought it would be good for Justin to meet somebody who knew what it was like to be thrust into the limelight at an early age. In October 2008, Justin signed to Usher's Island/Def Jam label.

Welcome to "My World"

Justin made his breakthrough as a mainstream artist in 2009. His debut single "One Time" reached the top 20 in Canada, the United States, France, and the United Kingdom. International chart success followed with his single "One Less Lonely Girl." Bieber fever was spreading fast ...

Justin—seen here in 2009 —had worldwide success with "One Time."

The summer of 2009 was filled with gigs, interviews, and TV appearances. When he wasn't performing, Justin was busy in the studio recording his debut EP (extended play) *My World*.

Justin worked with some of the top pop producers and writers in the business, including Usher and Tricky Stewart. When *My World* was released in the United States in November 2009, it sold 137,000 in its first week—a record for a new artist in that year.

Before the big performance for President Obama, Justin tweeted:

"Yeah, I'm nervous. If I mess up he might deport me back to Canada. Lol."

The year ended on a high note. Justin performed at the White House for President Barack Obama for "Christmas in Washington." Starring alongside Mary J. Blige, Neil Diamond, and Sugarland was a dream come true.

Usher with Justin at the Kids' Choice Awards in 2009.

Prince of Pop

Justin has become the idol of teenage girls all over the world. Crowds go crazy for him in what's been called "Bieber Fever."

Justin signs autographs for waiting fans at the London premiere of *Never Say Never*.

"I've seen an artist ascend this fast before but never this big. It's like the Beatles. It feels like when I was a kid and wanted to go see *A Hard Day's Night*."

Antonio "L.A." Reid, chairman of Justin's record label, Island Def Jam Music Group.

JUSTIN BIEBER
First Step 2 Forever My Story

Some of Justin's fans at a concert.

In November 2009, Bieber Fever hit the headlines. Over 3,000 fans turned up to see Justin at a shopping mall in Long Island. Some fans pushed their way to the front, and the situation became dangerous. The police arrested one fan and canceled the event. Justin didn't want to let his fans down, but he urged them to leave.

In April 2010, he was due to play a gig in Sydney, Australia. During the warm-up show, a couple of girls were injured when fans got out of control. Once again the show was canceled. Justin has admitted that he sometimes gets scared when he's surrounded by fans. It's just something he's had to get used to.

17

The Secret of Success

It takes more than a cute smile and a cool hairstyle to succeed in the music biz. Justin also happens to be a great musician with a fabulous voice. But what are the other things that make Justin such a sensation?

Justin is a professional. He loves his fans and doesn't want to let them down. Justin broke his foot during a gig in the UK in 2009. Rather than limp off stage, he finished the song.

Justin performing soon after breaking his foot in 2009.

18

Fame is hard for anyone to handle, but when you're a teenager, you need strong support. Family, friends, and a first-class management team help keep Justin's feet on the ground. Justin wants to be normal and having his friends around helps him to keep balance in his life. Justin is also a Christian. He says his faith helps him deal with stardom.

Smile, please! Justin jokes around with photograhers at a movie premiere.

In 2011, a lock of Justin's hair sold for $40,668 on the online auction site eBay. The money was donated to an animal welfare charity.

19

Not Just a Pretty Face

Justin is a mega sports fan. He's always played and followed basketball, football, and soccer. Recently he's gotten into playing golf. His number one love has always been hockey.

Justin training with Spanish soccer team, Barcelona, in 2011.

"It's kind of hard to balance school and work sometimes. But sometimes, like, if I'm going to the White House and I'm in there doing a tour and stuff, that's like school."

He's been playing hockey since he could walk and supports the Toronto Maple Leafs. The millions of fans who have been to see Justin live in concert know that he's a pretty nifty skateboarder, too!

Justin can do a Rubik's Cube in less than a minute and a half. And he's also pretty hot at Sudoku and chess! See him crack the Rubik's Cube on YouTube. www.youtube.com/watch?v=yEY7YA2MogY

In 2011, Justin played alongside Trey Songz and Romeo Miller in the BBVA NBA All-Star Celebrity Game.

Justin used to attend school in Stratford, Ontario. He didn't enjoy school and was often in trouble for talking in class. These days, a tutor travels with him everywhere he goes. He has to do three hours of home-schooling each day.

Girls! Girls! Girls!

> "Every one of my fans is so special to me ... It all happened because of you. I wake up knowing I have the best fans in the world ..."

It's no secret that Justin likes girls. But he tries to keep his personal life private.

Justin has a history of dating celebrity girls. He says it's best for him to go out with famous girls because they won't **idolize** him. Meanwhile, Justin tries hard to keep in touch with his female fans through the Internet. He has around 6.3 million followers on Twitter and 16.5 million friends on Facebook.

Beyonce and Justin pose together at the 2010 GRAMMY Awards.

Justin singing with "girlfriend" Selena Gomez in 2009. Justin likes a girl "who's funny, confident, and not afraid to be herself."

Justin says he's been obsessed with R&B star Beyonce since he was seven years old. He claims he was heartbroken when she married rapper Jay-Z. He describes her as "my celebrity crush," and calls her his ideal woman.

23

"Baby" and Beyond...

In 2010, Justin teamed up with rapper Ludacris on the single "Baby." The up-tempo dancepop song went to number one in France and reached the top ten across the world.

In early 2010, Justin released his first full-length album, *My World 2.0*. It mixes R&B, **hip-hop,** and pop sounds, and shows off Justin's astonishing vocal range. The album reached number one in the United States, Canada, and Australia, and climbed to number three in the United Kingdom.

Justin and Ludacris perform at the Help For Haiti concert in 2010.

In the summer of 2010, Justin began his first headline tour: My World Tour. He was on the road throughout 2010 and 2011 in the United States, Canada, Europe, Asia, Australia, and South America. In some places tickets sold out within minutes. The screaming fans were treated to an awesome show. Justin hovered above the crowd on a floating heart while singing hits like "Favorite Girl" and "Never Let You Go."

Justin's My World Tour featured guest singers including Miley Cyrus, shown here on left.

"I want to show that I love to perform. There are going to be some cool tricks, some electronic things that haven't been seen before, for sure."

21st Century Boy

Justin's life story so far was published in October 2010 in a book called *First Step 2 Forever, My Story*. Justin describes it as "my gift to you, the fans."

The book reveals more about Justin's rise to the top. There are never-before-seen photos and a taste of what it's like behind the scenes for the teen star.

"It's not really a concert movie, but it kind of shows my story. It was kind of cool to see myself so big, but at the same time I was a little ... what's the word? It made me feel self-conscious because your face is so big that you can see everything."

In February 2011, Justin starred in his first movie, called *Justin Bieber: Never Say Never*. The 3-D film is part-biopic and contains tons of concert footage. It also has more of those cute home videos of Justin as a youngster!

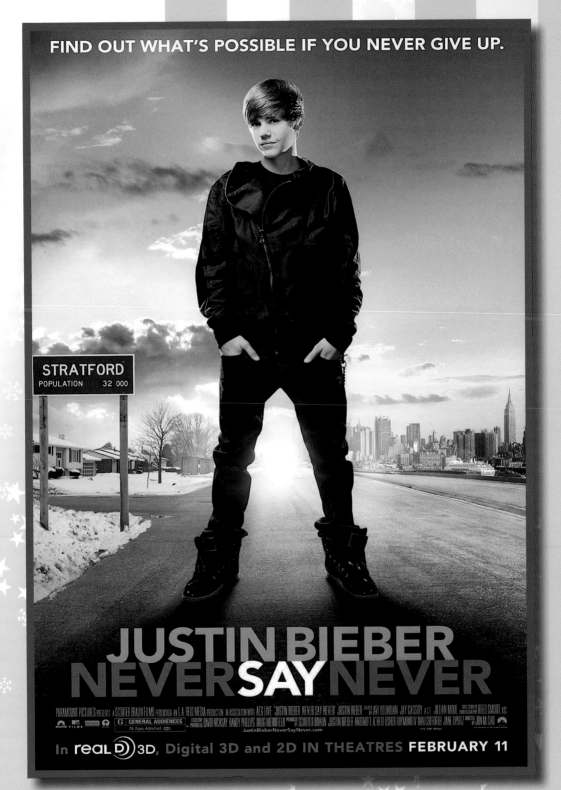

The poster for Justin's movie in 2011—which appeared on many feverish fans' bedroom walls!

Facing the Future

Justin appears with R&B megastars Boyz II Men on the *Dancing with the Stars* results show in 2011.

Justin was back in the studio in the summer of 2010. He began recording his follow-up to *My World 2.0*. Justin started writing songs while he was touring. Another exciting project was his 2011 Christmas album, *Under the Mistletoe*. Justin teamed up with his heroes Boyz II Men on one of the festive numbers.

During the next few years, he'll face his biggest challenge yet: leaping from teen star to an established performer. Since Justin's voice has broken, he hasn't been able to hit the same notes in "Baby." So at the moment, he is adapting his singing style to the changes in his voice.

Growing up in the media spotlight is tough, but Justin seems to have his feet on the ground. And he has enough musical talent to keep him in business for a long time to come!

Justin picks up two awards at the MTV Europe Music Awards 2011—for "Best Male" and "Best Pop."

"I'm a regular person. I'm living my dream and I'm just enjoying every minute of it."

Fan Guide

Full Name: Justin Drew Bieber

Date of Birth: March 1, 1994

Height: 5 feet 5 inches (1.65 meters)

Hometown: Stratford, Ontario, Canada

Record Label: Island, RBMG

Color of Eyes: Brown

Favorite Color: Purple

Favorite Food: Spaghetti Bolognese

There are many sites about Justin, and often they let you contribute to discussions about him. Remember, though, that it's OK to make comments, but it's not fair to be unkind. He cannot answer your comments himself!

www.justinbiebermusic.com/#!news

http://twitter.com/#!/justinbieber

www.facebook.com/JustinBieber

www.youtube.com/artist/justinbieber

www.justinbieberofficial.co.uk

www.justinbieberzone.com

http://www.mtv.com/music/artist/bieber_justin/artist.jhtml

www.last.fm/music/Justin+Bieber

March 1, 1994	Justin Bieber is born
2007–2008	Videos of Justin are uploaded onto YouTube by his mother
2008	Scooter Braun discovers Justin
	Signs to Island Records
2009	Debut single "One Day" is released
	Singles "One Less Lonely Girl," "Love Me," and "Favorite Girl" are released
	Starts the Urban Behavior Tour around Canada
	Performs at the White House for "Christmas in Washington"
2010	Guest presenter at the 52nd Grammy Awards
	Releases "Baby" the first single from *My World 2.0* album
	The singles "Eenie Meanie," "Somebody to Love," "U Smile," and "Pray" are released
	Debut album *My World 2.0* is released
	Kicks off his first headlining tour, My World Tour, in Hartford, Connecticut
	Guest stars in *CSI: Crime Scene Investigation*
	Performs on *X Factor* (UK)
	Wins MTV Europe Awards for Best New Act, Best Male, and Best Push Act
	Releases an album of acoustic songs called *My Worlds Acoustic*
	Nominated for four awards at the American Music Awards 2010 and wins them all—becomes the youngest person to win the Artist of the Year award
2011	*Justin Bieber: Never Say Never*, the concert/biopic of Justin's life is released
	Guest stars on *Dancing With The Stars*
	The album *Never Say Never—The Remixes* is released
	Releases the singles "Never Say Never" and "Mistletoe"
	Wins a Brit Award for the "International Breakthrough Act"
	Performs on *X Factor* (UK)
	Releases the Christmas album *Under the Mistletoe*
	Wins the Grammy for Best New Artist and Best Pop Vocal Album
	Wins MTV Europe Awards for Best Male, Best Pop, and Biggest Fans

Glossary

busk To perform or play music in a public place, usually for money.

debut The first appearance or performance of an artist.

demo A recording of an artist to find out how good they are at performing.

hip-hop An urban youth culture associated with rap music.

idolize To hero-worship or adore somebody.

phenomenon A remarkable and outstanding person or event.

R&B An African-American style of music that originates from rhythm and blues.

soul [music] A style of music that is influenced by gospel music and rhythm and blues.

Index